ANIMAL CHAMPIONS OF THE OCEAN

By William Anthony

KidHaven PUBLISHING

Published in 2023 by **KidHaven Publishing, an Imprint of Greenhaven Publishing, LLC**
29 East 21st Street
New York, NY 10010

Edited by: Emilie Dufresne
Designed by: Drue Rintoul

Cataloging-in-Publication Data

Names: Anthony, William, 1996-.
Title: Animal champions of the ocean / William Anthony.
Description: New York : KidHaven Publishing, 2023. |
Series: Animal champions | Includes glossary and index.
Identifiers: ISBN 9781534541535 (pbk.) | ISBN 9781534541559 (library bound) | ISBN 9781534541542 (6 pack) | ISBN 9781534541566 (ebook)
Subjects: LCSH: Marine animals--Juvenile literature. | Marine ecology--Juvenile literature.
Classification: LCC QL122.2 A58 2023 | DDC 591.77--dc23

Printed in the United States of America

CPSIA compliance information: Batch #CSKH23: For further information contact Greenhaven Publishing LLC, New York, New York at 1-844-317-7404.

Please visit our website, www.greenhavenpublishing.com.
For a free color catalog of all our high-quality books, call toll free 1-844-317-7404 or fax 1-844-317-7405.

Photo Credits

All images are courtesy of Shutterstock.com. With thanks to Getty Images, Thinkstock Photo and iStockphoto. Throughout – totally out, Romolo Tavani, Tainar. Front Cover – 3DMI, Martin Prochazkacz, Mike Price. 2–3 – Romolo Tavani. 4–5 – Vlad61, Willyam Bradberry. 6–7 – AshtonEa, Kjersti Joergensen. 8–9 – Rajat Kreation, Jennifer Mellon Photos, Ken Kiefer. 10–11 – pr2is, Aerial–motion. 12–13 – wildest-animal, lunamarina. 14–15 – RLS Photo, MilletStudio. 16–17 – William Farah, catalinaug, ACEgan. 18–19 – Tiago Sa Brito, valda butterworth, Kletr. 20–21 – cbpix, Jesus Cobaleda, stockpix4u. 22–23 – Kuznetcov_Konstantin, mimagephotography, Mike Flippo, Denis Moskvinov.

CONTENTS

Words that look like this can be found in the glossary on page 24.

IN THE OCEAN

Oceans are the huge parts of our planet that are covered in salty water. Some animals live at the top of the ocean, while others live in the cold, dark depths.

Let's meet the animal champions that call the ocean their home!

WHAT MAKES AN ANIMAL CHAMPION?

Animal champions don't always have to be the biggest, fastest, or strongest animals around. They are special because of the adaptations they have, or things they can do.

Are you ready? Let's dive into the ocean...

LEAFY SEA DRAGON

Leafy sea dragons are very difficult to spot. This is because they blend into their surroundings. When an animal looks like its surroundings, we say it is camouflaged.

Champion of Camouflage

Can you spot the leafy sea dragon?

Leafy sea dragons don't just keep predators away by blending in. They also have lots of spines on their bodies. These spines frighten off bigger fish that are looking for a tasty meal.

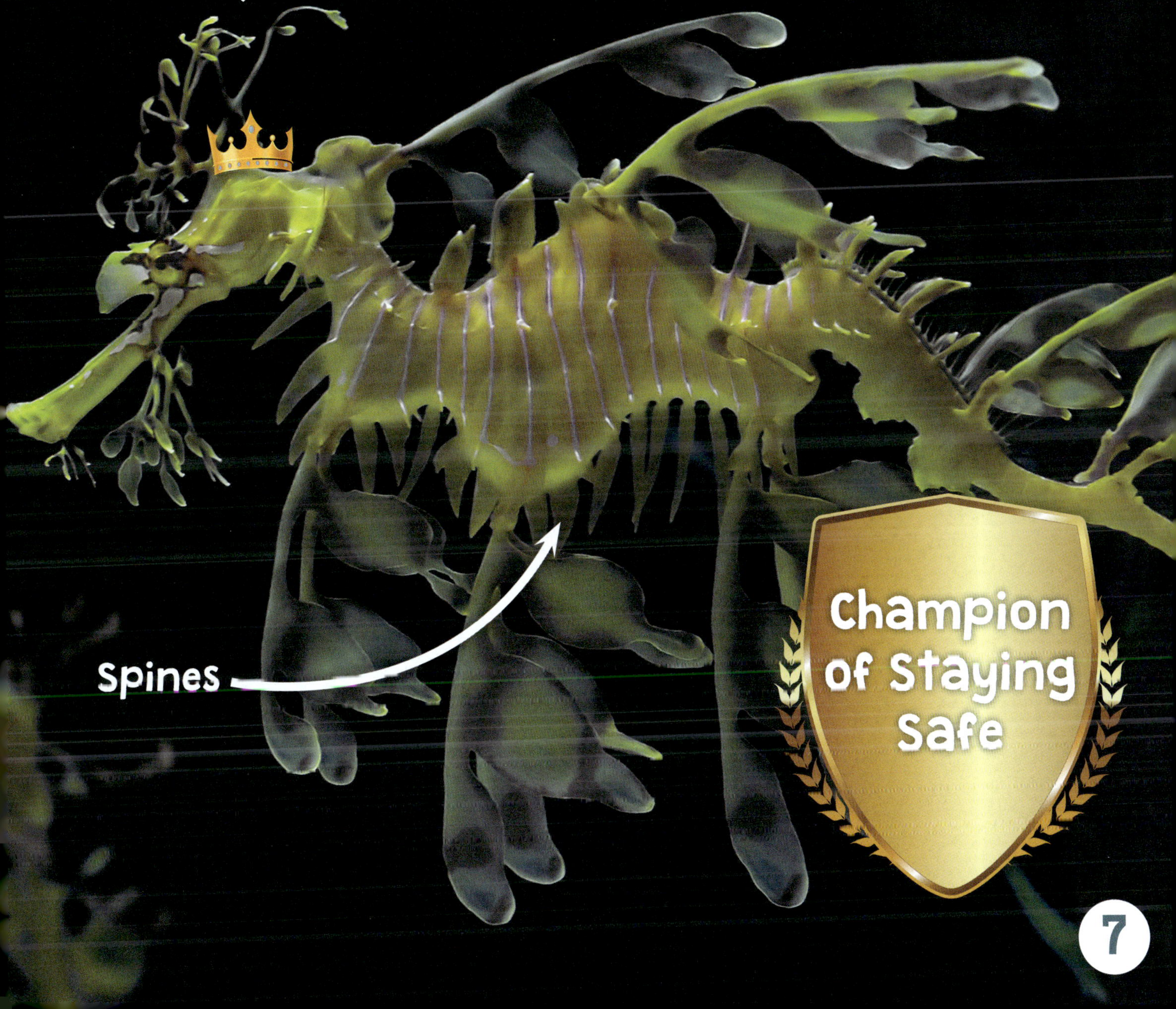

GREAT WHITE SHARK

The great white shark is one of the most dangerous animals in the ocean. It has around 300 sharp teeth and can speed through the water at around 15 miles (24 km) per hour!

Champion of Chomping

Great white sharks can also smell extremely well. They are thought to be able to smell <u>prey</u> almost 2 miles (3.2 km) away.

GIANT PACIFIC OCTOPUS

The giant Pacific octopus is the largest species of octopus on Earth. This octopus is very clever, and scientists have found out it can open jars and even solve mazes!

Champion of Challenges

The giant Pacific octopus has a sneaky way of tricking other animals. It can change color! The octopus can match the color of almost anything it is near to stay camouflaged.

This octopus has changed color to match the ocean floor.

Champion of Changing Color

SAILFISH

Sometimes, being an animal champion is all about being the best. The sailfish is one of the fastest fish in the ocean. It can swim at around 70 miles (113 km) per hour!

Sailfish live near the top of the ocean, but that doesn't mean they aren't super divers! Sailfish can dive down as deep as 1,150 feet (350 m) for food.

Champion of Deep-Sea Diving

LION'S MANE JELLYFISH

The lion's mane jellyfish has a scary way of catching its food. It has very long tentacles packed with deadly stinging cells, which it uses to shock the animals it eats.

Champion of Enormous Tentacles

The lion's mane jellyfish is the largest jellyfish on the planet. Its tentacles can grow up to 120 feet (37 m) long. That's taller than six giraffes stacked on top of each other!

LEATHERBACK TURTLE

What's the farthest you've ever traveled in one journey? The leatherback turtle travels more than 3,700 miles (6,000 km) for some journeys. These journeys are called migrations.

That distance is farther than the distance between London and New York City! Leatherback turtles make the journey between the places they feed and the places they lay their eggs.

Champion of Long-Distance Journeys

STARFISH

Starfish usually have five or more arms. For many animals, if they lose a limb, it is gone forever. However, starfish can grow back any arms that they lose! This is called regeneration.

Champion of Regeneration

Can you see which arm is regenerating?

Starfish eat in an amazing way. They push their stomachs out of their mouths and digest their food before pulling it inside their bodies.

CLOWNFISH

Have you ever helped someone else and they helped you back? Clownfish do this every day. Clownfish live in the tentacles of a strange animal called a sea anemone.

Anemone tentacles can sting other animals, but clownfish don't get hurt by them. By living in anemones, clownfish are protected from bigger fish. In return, clownfish clean anemones and bring them food.

Champion of Being Friends

BECOMING A CHAMPION

Let's see what animal adaptations we humans can use to be champions of the oceans!

You could put on a pair of flippers and be the fastest swimmer in the sea!

Strap on a snorkel and breathe underwater just like a fish.

Use a diving board to dive deep just like a sailfish.

Swim with a friend to stay safe just like a clownfish.

GLOSSARY

adaptations	changes that have happened to an animal over time that help them to be better suited to their environment
cells	the basic building blocks that make up all living things
deadly	able to cause something to die
digest	break down food for the body
limb	the arm, leg, or wing of an animal
predators	animals that hunt other animals for food
prey	animals that are hunted by other animals for food
species	a group of very similar animals or plants that can create young together
spines	sharp, pointed parts that stick out of an animal or plant
stomach	the sack-like part of the body through which food passes
surroundings	the places, conditions, or things that are around you

INDEX